BRITISH RAIL
in Camera
DR MICHAEL RHODES

Ten years of black and white railway photography by
members of the Cambridge University Railway Club

Oxford Publishing Company

Jeremy Hunns

Stewart Jolly

Above: members of the Cambridge University Railway Club, *left rear* Dr. Michael Rhodes, Kim Fullbrook, *front right* Paul Shannon (President).

The Cambridge University Railway Club (CURC)

'It occurred to us how much more amusing than cards, drinking and supper would be the formation of a new club, the meetings, of course, to be followed by supper.'

These words, although written of another Cambridge undergraduate club of slightly longer lineage than CURC, nonetheless epitomize the atmosphere of that vanished age. Like its venerable Oxonian counterpart, the University Railway Club originated at a time when railway enthusiasm would have been unthinkable, and when the social allure of a novel club seemed of paramount importance. It is odd to us today to find that characters as diverse as the novelist Evelyn Waugh and the politician R.A. Butler joined university railway clubs primarily because of the chance of lavish dinners in private restaurant cars. In Cambridge, this was a custom that continued until cost, and the abandonment of appropriate facilities, made it impossible. Judging from the present writer's experiences towards the end, some twenty five years ago, the occasion was by then a good deal less of a gourmet affair than it must have been in its heyday. And the environs of Hitchin Station, where the restaurant car waited during the speeches before being attached to the last 'down' train, were perhaps less than sybaritic.

This was one indulgence offered to the CURC when interest in railways was so unusual as to make the railway companies accommodating to an extent unbelievable today. Another was the provision of a locomotive, crew and branch line for a day, so that the undergraduates could fulfil their childhood dreams by becoming temporary engine drivers. Some fulfilled them more completely by becoming firemen and guards during the General Strike of 1926, a state of affairs almost as unimagineable. The annual engine driving remained a tradition into the 1960s, and has happily been revived in altered form using preserved steam of one kind or another. Looking back through the Club's old programme cards, it is constantly striking how willing the railway greats were to come down to address the small student groups. Old members will recall meetings in 16 Corpus, in Trinity Lecture Room, in St John's Music Room, at which one might listen to no less figures than Gresley himself, or Felix J.C. Pole of the GWR, or Cecil J. Allen, or George Dow. The process eventually became symbiotic, for a serious study of railways, whilst at university, and serious attention to the Club from the railway authorities, led young men and women to consider a railway career; and their subsequent interest in the Club caused the process to repeat itself.

This wasn't all. A well-informed and positively-critical public has become important to the continuation of the railway industry, and many students who have never contemplated employment in it are nonetheless enabled through experience at university to play a creative part in building public awareness of the need for a modern railway system. That is a major justification for the continuing generosity of railwaymen towards today's amateurs.

It is a long way removed from engine driving and banquets. The CURC, like the University itself, and the railway industry, has moved on from the Edwardian high summer when it all started. It is more earnest, dedicated and, as will be seen from this book, more professional. The meetings may no longer be 'followed by supper', but the members are still primarily in it because they want to enjoy themselves.

G.B. Skelsey
Assistant to the Vice-Chancellor
Vice-President CURC
University of Cambridge

Class 47 No. 47239 shunts the Metal Box factory at Wisbech on the occasion of a CURC visit on 9th June 1982. The CURC headboard was displayed by kind permission of the Railway Traffic Supervisor.

K. Fullbrook

A CURC group seen on a private railway, on 5th March 1982, operated by the Rugby Portland Cement Company at Barrington, near Cambridge. Locomotive No. 9 is seen propelling loaded wagons up to the works for distribution.

K. Fullbrook

Lincoln (Central) on 12th July 1984, and a 4-car diesel multiple unit leaves the station en route to the depot, headed by car No. 51299.

M. Rhodes

Typesetting by:
Colin Powell Typesetting & Design, Bournemouth, Dorset.

Printed in Great Britain by:
Biddles Ltd., Guildford, Surrey

Published by:
Oxford Publishing Co.
Link House
West Street
POOLE, Dorset

Dedication

To my wife, Jenny.

Frontispiece *(Right)*: A Birmingham to Hereford train crosses the River Severn at Worcester.

M. Rhodes

Foreword

I hope the reader will enjoy browsing through this collection of photographs taken by various members of the Cambridge University Railway Club (CURC). Photography has always been a prominent feature amongst the activities of the club, but in 1978, when the author arrived at Cambridge to study medicine, he had the unfortunate distinction of being the only entrant for the black and white category in the annual photographic competition. Michael Harris, editor of *Railway World*, was therefore forced to award him first prize! In subsequent years the competition has proved both a spur for undergraduates to take photographs and a focus on the last twelve months' photographic activity. Various well-known photographers such as Dick Blenkinsop, Rex Kennedy, Les Nixon and Colin Marsden have judged the competition in recent years. The author is grateful that the number of black and white entries has increased considerably, thus enabling the inclusion of ninety or so photographs taken by other members of the club.

This book resurrects an idea of a group of photographers from the CURC of twenty years ago. These men published their work under the pen-name of 'Fenman'. This volume provides the diesel equivalent to their steam album.

During my three years at Cambridge I found the formal meetings and trips arranged by the club very interesting. However, yet more enjoyable were the hours spent by the lineside with a good friend, Paul Shannon. Many was the day when we cycled to the TOPS office in order to ascertain the whereabouts of the Newmarket trip freight or one of the March to Temple Mills freights (*see pages 7 & 8*). We would either wait in the yard or cycle to one of our favourite locations nearby to capture the train on film. Frequent visits to various places in East Anglia were undertaken, one favourite being Peterborough, in the afternoon, to photograph the King's Cross to Hull and York expresses which were invariably hauled by a 'Deltic'. This was followed by a visit to March in time to see the last two freights of the week arrive from Tyne and Doncaster.

This tradition of outings in small groups continued well after the author left university and has borne much fruit as this album shows. The six contributors to this volume include two presidents of the CURC and all the prize winners from the photographic competitions of the last six years.

Now from the contributors to the contents. I have tried to include as wide a range of locations and motive power whilst still choosing pictures on their technical and artistic merit. Most contributors use 35mm equipment with a split between Canon and Olympus cameras, the author falling on the Canon side of the line. All of us are quite enthusiastic about using telephoto lenses, and this is evident in the selection of pictures. Freight trains make up half the photographs in the volume. This reflects an interest in this side of British Rail operations, and perhaps too much free time which has allowed members to sit for hours, waiting for the 'once weekly' freight!

In conclusion, may I thank all the photographers who have sent me pictures, and Geoffrey Skelsey for his 'potted' history of the CURC. Long may the tradition of photography flourish amongst the members of the CURC!

Dr Michael Rhodes
Newcastle
June 1986

Two Class 20 locomotives, Nos. 20019 and 20004 haul the 6T71 Hucknall to Toton freight at Bestwood Park on 2nd July 1985.
M. Rhodes

Class 37s around Cambridge

On 27th April 1984, No. 37113 waits for the 10.38 Doncaster to Cambridge diesel multiple unit to pass on the main line before bringing a train of oil empties off the remains of the former Mildenhall branch at Barnwell Junction, just north of Cambridge. This train, serving the BP oil depot, ran very infrequently. The photographer spent almost four years in Cambridge before getting this photograph, having seen the inward working just two days previously.

J. Hunns

Class 37 No. 37097 crosses the River Cam at Chesterton Junction to the north of Cambridge with the 8J93 16.10 March (Whitemoor) to Temple Mills freight. The train contains 46 wagons, making a total weight of 1,245 tons, which is near to the maximum tonnage for this train when hauled by a Class 37.

M. Rhodes

On 5th May 1981, a train of sand from Fen Drayton is hauled on to the main line by Class 37 No. 37047. The train which is classified as the 8B45, St. Ives to King's Cross working as it passes Chesterton Junction will assume Class 6 status after leaving Cambridge Yard.

M. Rhodes

Plate 1 (*Right*): On 25th May 1981, the 'Deltic Fenman' railtour was run for a second time, because of its initial popularity. Here, with the 'Deltic Fenman II' railtour, is Class 55 No. 55009, *Alycidon*. The air is filled with the 'Deltic' sound, and plenty of smoke, as the train accelerates north out of Cambridge Station.

M. Rhodes

(*Below*): The semaphores at Ely Dock Junction dominate this view of the 8J18 Bury St. Edmunds to Whitemoor freight. On 2nd June 1981 Class 37 No. 37102 hauls eight grain wagons at the start of their journeys to Birkenhead and Barry.

M. Rhodes

Plate 2: Grassmoor Junction signal box, in the middle of March Whitemoor Yard, controls the main line and the access for light locomotives from the 'up' hump. Here, Class 31 No. 31227 passes on the 'joint' line with the 7P04 Mansfield Coal Concentration to March working, on a cold and dull day in January 1981.

M. Rhodes

Plate 3: Gosberton, on the now closed March to Spalding 'joint' line, is the setting for Class 31 locomotives Nos. 31279 and 31217 as they head south with a train of scrap bound for March Whitemoor Yard on 7th May 1983.

J. Hunns

Plate 4: Class 31 No. 31189 takes the Royston line at Shepreth Branch Junction on a sunny day in June 1982. The train is bound for Barrington cement works, at Foxton.

J. Hunns

Plate 5: On 6th May 1981, the 8J44, Cambridge to Whitemoor service winds its way out of Cambridge Yard with a varied load of chemicals from ICI Duxford, and grain from Newmarket. The train is headed by Class 31 No. 31241.

M. Rhodes

Plate 6 (*Left*): Littlebury is the name of the area between Audley End Tunnels where this picture of the 14.52 Cambridge to Bishop's Stortford working was taken. The train is formed of a 2-car Cravens diesel multiple unit, Nos. 51273 and 56434, and was photographed on 9th April 1983.

P. Shannon

Plate 8 (*Right*): During the spring of 1981, the Leyland Experimental Vehicle (LEV) ran on several services in East Anglia. Here LEV-1 passes Coldhams Lane crossing with a special train from Ipswich to Cambridge.

M. Rhodes

Plate 9 (*Below Right*): A frosty morning on Coldhams Common to the north of Cambridge. The birds in the area take to the air as 2-car Cravens diesel multiple unit comprising cars 56137 and 51254 heads east to Newmarket.

P. Shannon

Plate 7 (*Below*): A panoramic view of Cambridge Station taken in January 1979. A diesel multiple unit, comprising cars 50578, 59218 and 50585, enters the station having crossed over from the uncovered track in the carriage sidings, visible on the right.

M. Rhodes

Plate 10: The 6S93 Harwich (Parkeston Quay) to Mossend working is seen passing Bury St. Edmunds, behind Class 40 No. 40135 on 10th June 1982. This train was regularly hauled by a Class 40 until the end of 1983. *M. Rhodes*

Plate 11: Another 'Speedlink' service from Harwich, the 6M98 to Warrington (Arpley Yard), is seen passing Soham on the Bury to Ely line. On this occasion, 10th June 1982, Class 37 No. 37105 hauls a train made up entirely of continental wagons. *M. Rhodes*

Plate 12: A sky full of semaphores provides the back-drop for Class 47 No. 47110 as it accelerates north through Ely with the 6M25 (TThO), Kennet to Mountsorrel stone train on 10th June 1982.

M. Rhodes

Plate 13: This view, photographed looking north from Cambridge in April 1979, shows the 8J21 12.22 Whitemoor to Temple Mills freight. Since the recent resignalling and track rationalisation at Cambridge, the two freight lines on the right of the picture have been removed, and the forest of semaphore signals has been replaced by a few modern colour-light posts. Class 37 No. 37092 heads mainly vacuum-fitted wagons, including a CGV grain wagon bound for Barry. The cement wagons (CPV) are bound for the Barrington cement works at Foxton, and the rest of the train is made up of coal from Nottinghamshire pits for distribution to the various Charrington's fuel depots between Cambridge and London. In the background Class 31 No. 31306 returns light engine from Newmarket.

M. Rhodes

Plate 14 (Above): The 09.40 London (Liverpool Street) to Harwich (Parkeston Quay) train accelerates through Mistley Station behind Class 47 No. 47577. As at many East Anglian stations, a fine combination of lineside telegraph poles, semaphore signalling and old station goods sidings provide additional railway interest.

P. Shannon

Plate 15 (Below): Class 25 No. 25123 provides unusual motive power for a Birmingham to Norwich express on 8th June 1979. The train is seen entering Norwich Station, the Class 31 allocated to work the train having failed at Birmingham.

M. Rhodes

Plate 16 (Above Right): In May 1982, Class 31 No. 31404 waits at London (Liverpool Street) with the 23.00 Liverpool Street to Norwich train. The photograph was taken when returning from the 50th Anniversary of the CURC's Oxford counterparts, the Oxford University Railway Society. To celebrate their half century and the demise of locomotive-hauled restaurant cars on the Western Region, the OURS arranged their annual dinner on the last such working out of Paddington.

J. Hunns

Plate 17 (Right): The 'double' home signal at Stanstead displays 'all clear' for an 'up' express, as Class 47 No. 47117 passes with the 08.35 London (Liverpool Street) to King's Lynn 'down', express on 9th April 1983.

P. Shannon

Plate 18: On 2nd April 1984, the snow lay 'deep and crisp and even' at Hatfield Peverel. Class 37s Nos. 37074 and 37053 pass 'wrong line' with a ballast train.

K. Fullbrook

Plate 19: The F&W Rail-tour's 'Essex Explorer' is pictured at Southminster behind Class 37 No. 37263, evidently photographed by quite a crowd on 19th March 1983.

K. Fullbrook

Plate 20: An unidentified High Speed Train passes Helpston to the north of Peterborough on the evening of 7th May 1983. The train is the 17.45 Leeds to King's Cross working.
K. Fullbrook

Plate 21: In an East Anglian scene that has changed little in twenty years, No. 31110 brings empty stock from Yarmouth to Norwich Crown Point Depot off the single line from Yarmouth to Reedham, via Berney Arms on 7th june 1984.
J. Hunns

Plate 22: The faded splendour of the station buildings at Felixstowe provide the setting for an afternoon departure to Ipswich. The train on 8th April 1983 is a 2-car Cravens diesel multiple unit comprising cars 51293 and 54131.
P. Shannon

Plate 25 (Above): A general view of Ipswich Yard, photographed from the north, shows Class 03 No. 03196 shunting a rake of BDVs. Directly above the Class 03 and partly hidden is Class 08 No. 08661, waiting to make the trip to the British sugar beet factory at Sproughton Lane, with a train of limestone from Wirksworth in Derbyshire.

M. Rhodes

Plate 23 (Above Left): A site soon to be transformed by electrification is Norwich (Thorpe) Station. On a sunny afternoon in June 1979, Class 47 No. 47004 awaits departure for London.

M. Rhodes

Plate 24 (Left): On 4th December 1980, the overhead catenary is highlighted in the low winter sun as Class 47 No. 47580 *County of Essex* accelerates past Stratford with the 10.30 express from London (Liverpool Street) to Norwich.

M. Rhodes

Plate 26 (Right): Class 40 No. 40158 winds its way out of the yard at March East with the 6S71, March to Paisley 'Speedlink' train. The VDA vans at the front of the train carry pet food for the dogs of Scotland, and have been brought down from Wisbech a couple of hours before this picture was taken on 29th May 1980.

M. Rhodes

Plate 28 (Above): The brickworks at Calvert used to send out bricks by rail to the Cory depot at Cardiff. The only remaining rail link with the works is used by the Greater London Council rubbish trains, one of which can be seen in the background. Passing the old Great Central station at Calvert on 22nd January 1983 are Class 25s Nos. 25205 and 25120 at the head of four UKF vans (PWA) from Akeman Street fertiliser depot, and bound for Bletchley.

M. Rhodes

Plate 29 (Below): A delightful branch line scene at Little Kimble on 7th April 1983, with the 8T16 Aylesbury to Princess Risborough freight hauled by Class 25 No. 25032 comprising three HEA coal hoppers and a guard's van (CAO). The coal hoppers will travel forward on the next stage of their journey attached to the 8V47 Princess Risborough to Acton freight.

P. Shannon

Plate 27 (Left): On 19th January 1983, the signal is at 'all clear', and the points are set for Class 25 No. 25086 to leave the Bletchley to Oxford line at Claydon LNE Junction on its journey south to Aylesbury. The train is the 6B04 Northampton to Aylesbury parcels.

M. Rhodes

Plate 30 (Above): Class 56 No. 56071 accelerates north past the carriage sidings at Oxford with the 6M55 Didcot to Toton merry-go-round service. The train comprises 43 HAA hoppers and, on 4th May 1982 was running two hours late.

M. Rhodes

Plate 31 (Below): Passing Port Meadow to the north of Oxford is Class 56 No. 56082. The local wildlife, including a heron, remains undisturbed by the passage of the 6E41 Didcot to Barrow Hill merry-go-round service.

M. Rhodes

Plate 32: Claydon L&NE Junction is the point at which the ex-Great Central main line used to cross the old Cambridge to Oxford cross-country route. Class 56 No. 56045 speeds past with the 6V38 Wolverton to Stoke Gifford stone train on 19th January 1983.

M. Rhodes

Plate 33: A busy scene at the south end of Banbury Station on 21 April 1982. Class 47 No. 47455 accelerates out of platform 3 with an 'up' express, while Class 56 No. 56105 waits in the loop with the 6V85 Toton to Didcot merry-go-round service. Standing between the two trains is a Marylebone service, and in the background Class 25 No. 25032 awaits its next duty.

M. Rhodes

Plate 34 (Left): The 13.39 Banbury to Marylebone service enters Princes Risborough on the old Great Central main line to London. On 19th January 1983 the train was made up of diesel multiple unit cars 51671, 59733, 59756 and 51677.

M. Rhodes

Plate 36 (Right): The brickworks at Stewartby form the backdrop for this view of a Bedford to Bletchley local service photographed on 28th July 1981. The diesel multiple unit is made up of cars 50390 and 56482. It looks as if the gatekeeper in the foreground has lost a button off his shirt!

P. Shannon

Plate 37 (Below Right): A Cardiff to Newcastle High Speed Train accelerates north out of Gloucester Station powered by cars 43187 and 43188. As well as the cathedral in the background are Class 50 No. 50023 at the head of the 3B42 Gloucester to Swindon parcels, and an unidentified Class 37 on a Severn Tunnel to Toton freight.

M. Rhodes

Plate 35 (Below): High Wycombe boasts an impressive array of semaphore signals, several of which are seen in this view of a Marylebone to Banbury train. Entering the station from the south on 25th March 1983 is a diesel multiple unit, comprising cars 51873, 59763, 59656 and 51670. This formation will depart as the 10.18 to Banbury.

M. Rhodes

Plate 38 (Above Left): The sidings at Quedgeley, south of Gloucester serve the Dowmac Company who make concrete sleepers, a trainload of which can be seen in the yard. Various other concrete beams are also produced at this plant. On 29th November 1983 Class 08 No. 08836 enters the yard on its daily trip from Gloucester New Yard. The line in the foreground leads to MOD property and, at the moment is disused.

M. Rhodes

Plate 40 (Above): An overcrowded Banbury Yard is host to, (from left to right), Class 25 No. 25198, Class 45 No. 45034, Class 25s Nos. 25181 and 25279, Class 40 No. 40057 and Class 08 No. 08740. Later in the evening of 13th May 1983, Class 40 No. 40057 and Class 25 No. 25198 double-headed the 9T36 18.00 Banbury to Bescot freight. The Class 40 came south the night before at the head of the 4Z46 Stockton to Southampton Freightliner. Incredibly, eleven months later, the yard was closed.

M. Rhodes

Plate 41 (Below): The entry to Rewley Road coal depot in Oxford is controlled by a manually-wound swing-bridge. Here, on 16th March 1983, the Oxford shunting staff wind the bridge round to allow Class 08 No. 08804 to enter with its load of four MCVs containing coal.

M. Rhodes

Plate 39 (Left): Gloucester Docks on the Sharpness canal still have a wharf-side rail link. Here, on 12th December 1983, Class 08 No. 08836 arrives with three 'Polybulks' carrying grain for export from the docks. The grain originates in East Anglia and, after travelling west on the 6V85 19.47 March to Severn Tunnel 'Speedlink' service, it is brought to Llantony Wharf on a trip from Gloucester New Yard.

M. Rhodes

Plate 44: Much of the character of Worcester (Shrub Hill) Station is captured in this view of Class 31 No. 31234 as it leaves for Birmingham with its load of two parcel vans. The train is bound for Curzon St. Parcel Depot, and was photographed on 25th April 1985.

M. Rhodes

Plate 42 (Above Left): The morning Newcastle to Cardiff express crosses the River Severn, to the south of Gloucester, near Over Junction. The driver of High Speed Train, No. 253040, can clearly be seen in the afternoon sun of 15th December 1983.

M. Rhodes

Plate 43 (Left): On an icy cold day in February 1985, HST No. 43135 eases over the Worcester to Bir-mingham Canal between Worcester (Foregate Street) and Worcester (Shrub Hill) stations. Spare capacity in the middle of the day has allowed the Western Region the luxury of providing an HST for the Cotswold and Malvern express on a line which is often regarded as a secondary route.

M. Rhodes

Plate 45: Dunhampstead level crossing is on the main NE/SW route near Droitwich. It is one of the few surviving manually-operated crossings on this busy main line. The character of the signal box, with its large wheel for closing the gates, is enhanced by the signalman's quaint habit of strapping carpet to his shoes to keep the floor of the box clean!

M. Rhodes

Plate 46: Class 47 No. 47534 enters Leamington Spa Station in the middle of a torrential downpour at the head of a Newcastle to Poole express. The nose of Class 50 No. 50010 can be seen on the left; it heads a Paddington to Liverpool train. This service had to be diverted via Solihull as the storm had damaged the track circuits at Kenilworth, thus putting the signals out of action for much of the afternoon.

M. Rhodes

Plate 47: The 8V33 Banbury to Oxford working used to trip south three afternoons each week carrying coal dropped at Banbury Yard by the Toton to Eastleigh freight. Passing under the road bridge at Jericho is Class 25 No. 25321 at the head of a mixed load on 28th May 1982. This service has been replaced by a through 'Speedlink' service from Bescot each morning.

M. Rhodes

Plate 48: On 25th May 1982, Morris Cowley, Oxford still had its signal box, although the signals had been removed some months before. Here Class 31 No. 31152 leaves the yard with the 4M32 air-braked freight to Bescot Down Storage Sidings. The wagons behind the locomotive (PKA) are only two days old and are on their first revenue-earning run. The yard pilot is Class 08 No. 08946.

M. Rhodes

Plate 49: A pair of Class 37s, Nos. 37295 and 37181 approach Swanbourne, west of Bletchley on the line to Oxford. On 3rd February 1983, the 6V38 Wolverton to Stoke Gifford working is made up mainly of the newer high-sided stone wagons. In the background the Bletchley flyover can just be made out to the left of the brickworks chimneys.

M. Rhodes

Plate 50 (Left): A busy scene at Pengam Freightliner Terminal, Cardiff. On 1st June 1983 Class 56 No. 56037 backs part of its train, the 4S81 19.45 Pengam to Glasgow working, into the loops at Pengam. Partially obscured by its exhaust, Class 47 No. 47146 arrives with the 4C48 18.15 Bristol to Pengam train. Traffic from Bristol is then attached to the long-distance trains which leave Cardiff in the evening.

M. Rhodes

Plate 51 (Above): Shortly after this picture was taken on 23rd September 1983, the sleeper service from Milford Haven to Paddington was withdrawn from the timetable, thus obviating the need to haul the sleeping car down to Milford each tea time. Class 33 No. 33039 crosses the River Loughor hauling the 14.50 Swansea to Milford Haven express with the sleeping car placed second in the formation.

J. Hunns

Plate 52 (Below): High Speed Train No. 253034 speeds west past Neath with the 10.00 Paddington to Swansea express. This view was photographed from the old station at Neath and Brecon Junction on 2nd December 1983.

M. Rhodes

Plate 53 (Above): Using a 500mm mirror lens accentuates the irregularity of the South Wales main line seen in the right foreground. Two 3-car Derby diesel multiple units crawl through the carriage washer at Cardiff Canton Shed on 7th January 1984. Although the shed is half a mile away it is seen quite clearly with this powerful lens.

M. Rhodes

Plate 54 (Below): The terminus at Cardiff (Bute Road) lies largely derelict with only the occasional local train to Coryton disturbing the rust and sparrows. A 3-car Derby diesel multiple unit, No. C315, awaits departure with its solitary passenger on 10th September 1983. The train is the 12.37 to Coryton.

M. Rhodes

Plate 55 (Above Right): Radyr Station, just south of the Taff Gap, is a busy junction, with a large yard to the south. All is, however, quiet on a December afternoon in 1977 as diesel multiple unit No. C452 pauses with a Treherbert to Barry Island train.

M. Rhodes

Plate 56 (Below Right): Passengers detrain at Dinas Powys from a Merthyr to Barry Island local service on 30th December 1983.

M. Rhodes

Plate 57 (Above): The Abercwmboi furnacite plant generates most of the traffic to traverse the Aberdare branch. Here, on Saturday, 26th March 1983, Class 08 No. 08350 draws HTV hoppers, loaded with steaming coke nuts, from the ovens.

M. Rhodes

Plate 58 (Below): The Burry Port & Gwendraeth Valley line is now closed between Kidwelly Junction and Burry Port. In this view, photographed on 15th September 1983, shortly before closure, Class 03s Nos. 03144, 03151 and 03120 pass the site of Pembrey Station with a train of coal bound for Burry Port Yard.

M. Rhodes

Plate 59 (Above): A tired British Railways guard trudges home from Newport Station as Class 37 No. 37281 heads east with the 7A98 Ebbw Vale to Severn Tunnel freight. The train carries mainly plated steel coil on BBA wagons but also has two empty flat wagons (SOA and SPA) at the front of the formation.

M. Rhodes

Plate 60 (Below): Class 37 No. 37227 indulges in a little lunchtime shunting at Tondu on 22nd December 1981. Having placed eight MDVs, (21 ton mineral wagons) in a siding for Maesteg, it here removes twenty MDVs which it will take up the valley to Ogmore washery.

M. Rhodes

Plate 63 (Above): Class 40 No. 40035 crosses the River Usk to the north of Newport with the 6S78 18.10 Severn Tunnel to Mossend 'Speedlink' working. On 5th August 1983, the train contains, amongst its varied load, four Tiger Leasing Ltd. china clay wagons.

M. Rhodes

Plate 61 (Above Left): Severn Tunnel Junction Yard is the 'Speedlink' capital of South Wales with nearly eighty 'Speedlink' services in and out each day. On 11th August 1983, Class 45 No. 45075 leaves with the 6E64 service to one of the most distant destinations, Haverton Hill on Teeside.

M. Rhodes

Plate 62 (Left): The first re-liveried Class 56, No. 56036, leads Class 56 No. 56044 at the head of the 6C68 empty iron-ore train from Llanwern to Port Talbot. The train was photographed on 2nd June 1983 to the west of Ebbw Junction, Newport.

M. Rhodes

Plate 64 (Right): The points at Cwmgorse Branch Junction have just been changed by the guard of the Pantyffynnon to Gwaun-Cae-Gurwen coal empties. On 1st April 1982, this train was hauled by Class 37 No. 37302 and composed of MDO mineral wagons.

K. Fullbrook

Plate 65: Pothkerry Viaduct stretches across Porthkerry Park, just west of Barry, on the Vale of Glamorgan line. On 22nd July 1983, a pair of Class 37s work hard up the gradient with a merry-go-round train which they will deposit in the reception sidings at Aberthaw.

M. Rhodes

Plate 66: The railway to Onllwyn runs parallel to the A465 road and under the South Wales main line at Neath and Brecon Junction. Class 37s Nos. 37162 and 37300 head the 7C93 Blaenant to Aberthaw merry-go-round working. The train is restricted to a maximum speed of 45m.p.h. when loaded, but is allowed to travel at 60m.p.h. when empty. This photograph was taken on 2nd December 1983 when it was seen passing the signal box at Neath & Brecon Junction.

M. Rhodes

Plate 67 (Right): China clay loaded in vacuum-fitted UCV wagons pass under the Cornwall main line at Coombe. Class 37 No. 37299 heads the train on its journey from Moorswater to Fowey Docks on 12th June 1980.

P. Shannon

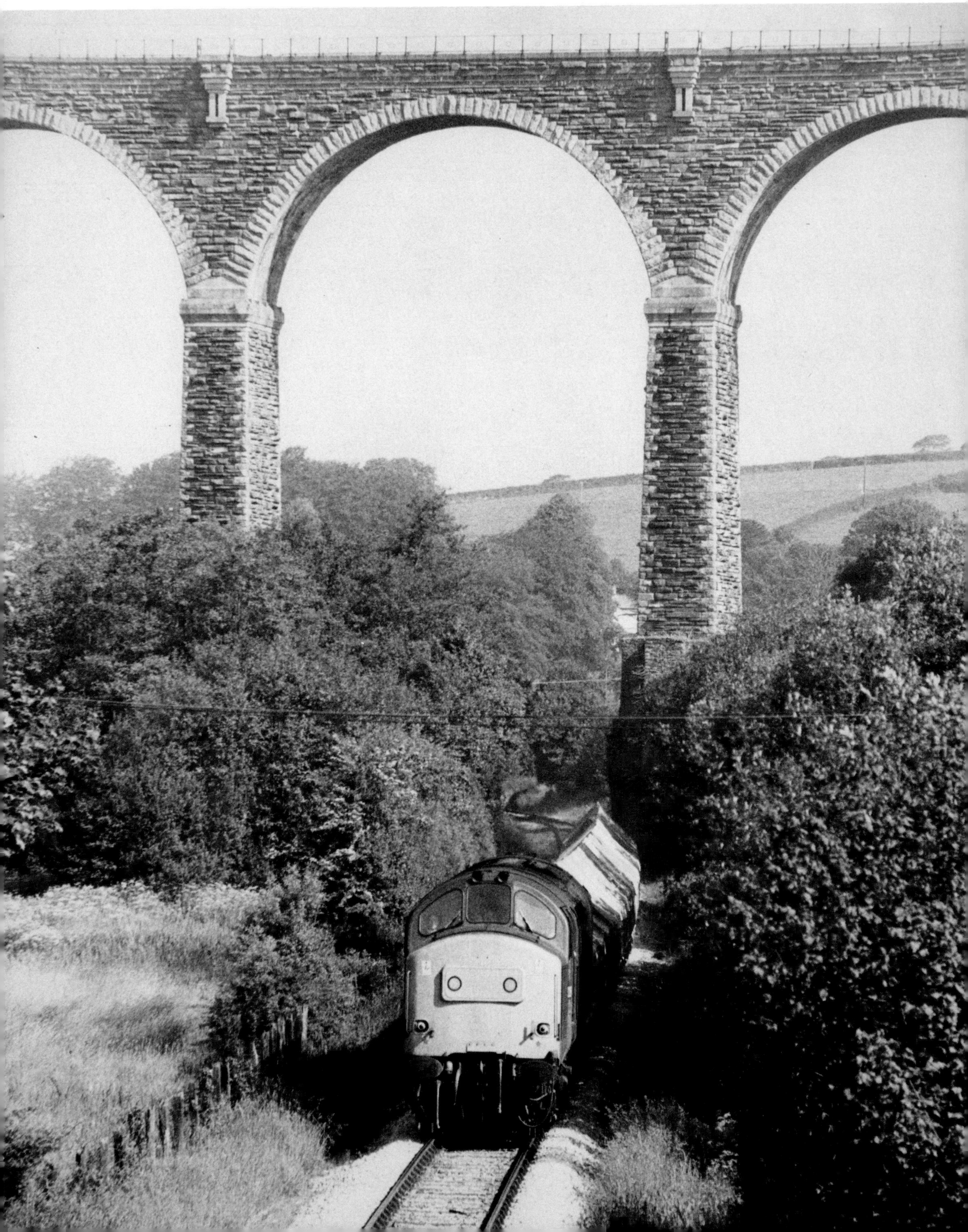

Plate 68 (Above): The full rural splendour of the long and winding branch to Wenford Bridge is illustrated in this view of Class 08 No. 08113. Its load of 56 empty UCV wagons had been brought as far as Boscarne Junction the previous day.

P. Shannon

Plate 70 (Above Right): A gantry of Great Western lower quadrant semaphores signals at Newton Abbot is used to frame the 6C39 09.32 St. Blazey to Severn Tunnel Junction 'Speedlink' service. Class 47 No. 47373 hauls a ferry van, one VEA van, one Tiger leasing wagon containing china clay bound for Mossend, and an empty HEA hopper, quite a mixture for such a short train.

M. Rhodes

Plate 71 (Below Right): With mountains of china clay waste in the background, Class 47 No. 47298 winds its way along the Drinnick Mill branch on 5th August 1982. The train is a trip freight from Drinnick Mill to St. Blazey Yard and carries china clay bound for the continent.

P. Shannon

Plate 69: Class 46 No. 46028 stands at the head of the 6C43 14.45 St. Blazey to Severn Tunnel Junction 'Speedlink' train. The first three wagons are bound for Modane and Basle, via Dover. The Tiger Leasing china clay wagon is bound for Cliffe Vale, in Stoke on Trent, the VDA van for Mossend, and the five PRA wagons at the end of the train for Corpach, on the West Highland line.

M. Rhodes

Plate 72 (Above): Under a stormy sky on 16th September 1983, Class 33 No. 33001 passes Hawkeridge Junction on the northern approach to Westbury. The train is the 16.10 Bristol (Temple Meads) to Portsmouth Harbour service.

S. Jolly

Plate 73 (Below): A local passenger service from Plymouth to Penzance is framed by the entrance to Loswithiel goods shed on 3rd August 1982. The train is hauled by Class 50 No. 50047, still in its old livery at this time.

P. Shannon

Plate 74 (Above): The refuelling shed at Bristol (Bath Road) Depot is now used as a diesel multiple unit maintenance depot. On the night of 4th May 1984, all three roads were occupied by units C811, B433 and B577.

M. Rhodes

Plate 75 (Below): At the southern extremity of the rail network is Penzance Station. At 22.00 on 14th July 1980, HST unit No. 253002 waits to run to Long Rock Depot for refuelling, and Class 50 Nos. 50010 and 50006 are stabled in the station.

M. Rhodes

Plate 76: The 15.43 Par to Newquay train is seen just north of St. Blazey. On 29th July 1983, the train was formed of diesel multiple unit cars 51320, 59472 and 51305.

M. Rhodes

Plate 78 (Above Right): With the closure of Acton Yard in May 1984, came the cancellation of the 7A01 Oxford to Acton freight service. This was regularly hauled by a Class 50, and here No. 50015 shunts the train in Didcot Yard in the shadow of the power-station.

M. Rhodes

Plate 77: Another rural scene, this time on the Looe branch. Here, diesel unit No. 55026 forms the 10.05 Looe to Liskeard working, on 2nd August 1982.

P. Shannon

Plate 79: In June 1976, the author put his first roll of film through his first SLR camera, a Practika. One of the pictures taken was this one of Class 50 No. 50009 passing Dawlish Warren with a 'down' express.

M. Rhodes

Plate 80: The fine array of semaphores at Taunton provides the setting for this picture of Class 50 No. 50013 accelerating out of the station with a 'down' express on 19th July 1980.

M. Rhodes

The South

Plate 81: On 29th April 1983, the 6W86 Poole to Eastleigh freight was made up of only four wagons, two carrying explosives and two acting as barrier wagons. The two VDA vans in the centre of the formation originate from the Winfrith siding, near Wool. Class 33 No. 33101 restarts the train after a short signal stop at Bournemouth Station.

M. Rhodes

Plate 82: Three years earlier than the scene in *Plate 81*, a pair of Class 33 locomotives, Nos. 33103 and 33008, reverse a lengthy Poole to Eastleigh freight into the yard at Eastleigh. The train is much longer, because of the large amount of traffic from the goods yard at Poole which closed in 1983. Also the train is completely vacuum-braked, whereas in 1983 the transition to air-braked wagons was complete on the Southern Region.

M. Rhodes

Plate 83: The impressive signal gantry at the west end of Southampton Station forms the frame for this picture of Class 33 No. 33045 at the head of an oil train from Fawley Oil Refinery. The gantry has recently disappeared in the resignalling of the area.

M. Rhodes

Plate 84: The carriage of nuclear waste by rail was much in the news during 1984. In July, a special 100m.p.h. crash was arranged by British Rail and the CEGB to test the strength of the flasks used to transport waste from power-stations around the country to Windscale, in Cumbria. Here, an empty flask returns to Dungeness Power-Station in Kent, hauled by Class 33 No. 33206. The train was photographed on 25th August 1983 passing Lydd Town Station.

P. Shannon

Plate 85 (Left): A Waterloo to Exeter express winds its way out of London's largest terminus on 24th September 1983. The train is hauled by Class 50 No. 50028 providing 2,700hp for the journey west, via Salisbury.

M. Rhodes

Plate 86 (Above): Passengers from Portsmouth to Cardiff used to travel as far as Bristol in a diesel electric multiple unit like the example seen here; the final leg of their journey being undertaken by diesel multiple unit. Since 1980, when this picture was taken, much has changed. Locomotive-hauled trains ply the Portsmouth to Cardiff route, and signals like these at St. Deny's have been replaced by colour lights.

M. Rhodes

Plate 87 (Left): The lunch-time Poole to Leeds express winds its way into Poole Station after its two hour sojourn in the carriage sidings. Class 47 No. 47515 coasts into the station, and Class 33 No. 33101 waits in the background with the 6W86 Poole to Eastleigh freight (*see Plate 81*).

M. Rhodes

Plate 88 (Left): Class 6L diesel electric multiple unit No. 1031 passes the rural setting of Etchingham Station with the 15.45 Charing Cross to Hastings express. Because of the clearance of several tunnels on this line, the multiple units have a slightly narrower profile than the rest of rolling stock used on British Rail.

R. Nelson

Plate 90 (Right): The imposing structure of Canterbury East signal box dominates this view of a long 'Speedlink' freight made up mainly of ferry wagons. The train is the 6V40 08.45 Dover Town to Acton Yard working, hauled by electro-diesel Class 73 No. 73109.

P. Shannon

Plate 89 (Below Left): Once again a fine array of semaphore signals is used to good effect in this picture of the 09.37 Eridge to Tonbridge working. Diesel electric multiple unit No. 1305 passes Tunbridge Wells West Station on 23rd August 1983.

P. Shannon

Plate 91 (Below): Another Class 73, No. 73132, passes the lines of electric multiple units stored at Selhurst Depot in south London. Its load is engineer's traffic bound for New Cross Gate Yard.

K. Fullbrook

Plate 94 (Right): The LNWR signal box at Wooferton used to control the branch from the main Hereford to Shrewsbury line across to Cleobury Mortimer. Class 33 No. 33042 rattles past with a Crewe to Cardiff express on 28th May 1985. With the recent rerouting of Manchester to Cardiff trains along this line, it has re-entered the list of inter-city routes after an absence of fifteen years.

M. Rhodes

Plate 92: A Gloucester 3-car diesel multiple unit is headed by power car No. W51098 as it leaves Dorking Town with the 10.16 Reading to Tonbridge cross-country service on 22nd August 1983.

R. Nelson

Plate 93: The empty signal gantry at Kensington Olympia testifies to more prosperous times, as a cross-London transfer freight from Acton Yard to Norwood Yard passes by. The train is made up mainly of HTV hoppers, carrying coal, and is hauled by Class 50 No. 50024.

P. Shannon

Plate 95: The author visited Lichfield on 9th March 1984, just one week before the line to Walsall closed. Although there were very few freight trains running on that day, the signals at Lichfield City Station made a fine picture. A mid-morning train to Longbridge stands under the ornate canopy awaiting departure with a few shoppers.

M. Rhodes

Plate 96: A fine study in light and shade at Birmingham (New St.), on 14th September 1983, of Class 50 No. 50047 *Swiftsure* backing on to the 09.20 Liverpool (Lime St.) to Penzance train for the diesel-hauled part of the journey.

S. Jolly

Plate 97 (Above Right): The M6 motorway crosses the NE/SW main line at Bromford Bridge. With power car No. 43189 trailing, a 'down' express whistles past the soon to disappear signal box at Bromford Bridge. This controls the entrance to the Esso oil sidings at this location.

M. Rhodes

Plate 98 (Right): Two single car diesel units, Nos. 55000 and 55004, leave Claverdon with the 11.50 Stratford-upon-Avon to Leamington Spa service, on 27th October 1984.

P. Shannon

Plate 101 (Right): A trip freight from the British Levland factory at Longbridge approaches its destination of Washwood Heath Yard behind Class 25 No. 25283. The eight wagons which make up the load will be tripped to Bescot Yard later on the 2nd March 1984.   M. Rhodes

Plate 102 (Below Right): Washwood Heath No. 5 signal box is one of three manual boxes which control the sidings in the Washwood area. The main line is controlled by the panel box at Saltley. This view shows Class 47 No. 47186 reversing the 6T78 Ironbridge to Daw Mill merry-go-round train into the yard. The train is being stabled for inspection of a hot box and a crew change. The lines converge in the foreground to what was the old hump, but what is now just used as the western access to the yard.

M. Rhodes

Plate 99: The only train to traverse the Lichfield to Walsall freight line during daylight hours on 9th March 1984 was the 9Z80 from Boston Docks to Wedensfield Steel Terminal in Wolverhampton. It is pictured passing Rushall Crossing hauled by a pair of Class 20s, Nos. 20180 and 20185. The steel coil is being carried on BEV vacuum-fitted bogie bolsters.

M. Rhodes

Plate 100: On 11th September 1980, four KEV wagons, loaded with steel wire from the GKN steelworks in Cardiff, for a light load for Class 47 No. 47344 on the 6T30 Bescot to Wedensbury trip freight. The train is seen leaving the main Stourbridge line at Wedensbury Station. The photograph was actually taken from a bridge that used to carry the old Great Western main line to Birmingham (Snow Hill) and Paddington.

M. Rhodes

Plate 104 (Left): Class 47 No. 47192 crosses the River Severn at Ironbridge with the 6E32 09.03 Ironbridge to Barrow Hill empty merry-go-round working, on 10th August 1982.

P. Shannon

Plate 103 (Left): During 1980, there were daily special trains of iron ore from Shotton Steelworks to Llanwern. These were run in order to clear the stockpile of ore left at the North Wales site after the cessation of steel production at the plant. Approaching Shrewsbury on 30th September 1980 are Class 56 locomotives Nos. 56033 and 56038 with such a train.

M. Rhodes

Plate 105 (Below Left): On 30th September 1980, the 7J36 Coton Hill Yard to Bescot freight was most unusually hauled by a pair of Class 20s. Nos. 20041 and 20031 pass through Shrewsbury Station at the start of their journey.

M. Rhodes

Plate 106: The Christmas mail is unloaded at Craven Arms Station on 16th December 1980. Multiple leaks from the steam heating are highlighted, as Class 25 No. 25042 waits for the off.

M. Rhodes

Plate 107 (Left): Enterprising local residents have started a coffee shop on Malvern Station. Here, pupils from the neighbouring public schools meet for coffee. On 5th February 1985, it is far too cold to sit outside. However, the ornate tables and chairs provide an interesting foreground in this picture of diesel multiple unit No. L411 forming a Birmingham (New Street) to Hereford passenger service.

M. Rhodes

Plate 109 (Right): One of the most impressive pieces of railway civil engineering in the country is the Harringworth arches. They stretch over one mile across the River Welland and carry the old Midland main line on its way from Manton Junction to Glendon Junction. On 14th November 1983, Class 45 No. 45043 *The King's Own Royal Border Regiment* hauls a short rake of MXV scrap wagons to the dismantled steelworks at Corby. The train is the 7T32 Toton to Corby freight.

M. Rhodes

Plate 108 (Below): The station at Henley in Arden retains this magnificent Great Western footbridge along with a station sign and signalling from previous, more prosperous, days. On 9th April 1985, diesel unit No. 53071 heads a 3-car set which forms the 17.50 Stratford to Birmingham (Moor Street) local service.

M. Rhodes

Plate 110: As reported in the railway press, the signal box at Glendon East was destroyed by fire on 23rd April 1984. On 3rd July 1983, a pair of Class 45s Nos. 45150 and 45108, pass with the diverted (Sundays only) 13.05 Nottingham to St. Pancras express. After twenty years without a local passenger service, it is interesting to reflect on the varied plans currently being put forward for a new passenger service to Corby.

P. Shannon

Plate 111: On 26th July 1979, at Wellingborough, Class 45 No. 45077 stands on the slow lines awaiting a crew change for its cement train. On the right, Class 45 No. 45137 hurtles through the station with a St. Pancras to Sheffield express.

M. Rhodes

Plate 112: The new signalman stokes the fire at Manton Junction signal box as the old one prepares to leave on his moped. Class 45 No. 45026 emerges from the tunnel at the head of the 9T32 Toton to Corby pick-up freight. This train was down graded to a 'T' or trip freight in May 1983.

M. Rhodes

Plate 113: At Corby, the signal gantry casts its shadow on to the bonnet of Class 45 No. 45147. Its varied load is the 8X76 Toton to Temple Mills freight. As the train passed it was not entirely obvious why it was classified 'X' for 'out of gauge load' as all the wagons appeared to be normal in size.

M. Rhodes

Plate 114 (Above): The Mark IId coaches of a St. Pancras to Sheffield express are highlighted in the evening sun as they are whisked past Tibshelf behind Class 47 No. 47576. The line to the left curves around to Westhouses Depot, whilst the wagons in the background are in Alfreton goods depot.

M. Rhodes

Plate 115 (Below): A short merry-go-round trip, the 6T98 Drakelow to Rawdon working, enters the colliery at Rawdon. This scene has been transformed, since this picture was taken in December 1981, by considerable mining subsidence. The main line in the foreground now has a large dip in it.

M. Rhodes

Plate 116 (Above): Tuxford is the point on the East Coast Main Line where the branch to High Marnham Power-Station crosses. An HST (power cars 43079 and 43090) speeds south at over 100m.p.h. with a King's Cross-bound express on 11th July 1984.

M. Rhodes

Plate 117 (Below): Passing through the beautiful Derbyshire countryside just south of Ambergate is the 08.08 Newcastle to Plymouth express. On 15th April 1983, HST unit No. 253049 takes passengers on their journey south.

R. Nelson

Plate 118 (Above Left): A tamping machine, and various wagons requiring repairs, pass the south end of Toton Yard on their way to the wagon repair shops on the right of the picture. The trip freight is hauled by Class 20 No. 20181 running 'nose' first, and was captured on film in June 1981.

M. Rhodes

Plate 119 (Left): A train of assorted mineral wagons passes the disused sidings at Tibshelf on its way from the Avenue carbonisation plant, near Chesterfield, to Condor Park Sidings. A pair of Class 20s, Nos. 20162 and 20155, brings the load past what is now a new stabling point. The yard was brought back into use in May 1984 because of the closure of Westhouses Depot and the sale of adjacent land to the National Coal Board. *M. Rhodes*

Plate 121 (Right): Class 20s are a fairly common site on passenger trains during the summer months, and particularly on Saturdays. Two examples of the class, Nos. 20157 and 20135, approach Wainfleet with the 08.38 (Saturdays only) Leicester to Skegness working.
S. Jolly

Plate 120 (Above): Coal from Hucknall Colliery arrives at Toton behind Class 20s Nos. 20196 and 20016, on 3rd June 1981. The train will reverse into the reception sidings, seen on the far left in this picture.

M. Rhodes

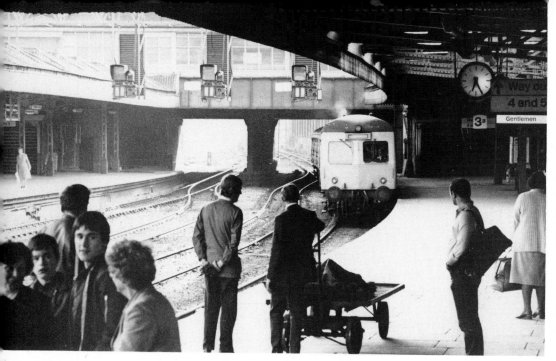

Plate 122: A group of schoolboys and several other passengers wait on the platform at Nottingham (Midland) Station for the train to Lincoln. In time-honoured fashion, one of the schoolboys gazes vacantly towards the photographer rather than towards the train where he is 'supposed' to be looking. A diesel multiple unit, comprising cars 50714, 59293 and 50678, form this evening Crewe to Lincoln cross-country service.

M. Rhodes

Plate 123: A beautifully-framed picture of the 08.58 Boston to Doncaster service passing Potterhansworth signal box on 16th April 1983.

R. Nelson

Plate 124: Wrawby Junction, to the west of Barnetby, has a large collection of semaphore signals, one of which is used to frame this view of a diesel multiple unit comprising cars 54018 and 53008. It is running from Doncaster to Cleethorpes with a local passenger service, on 13th July 1984.

M. Rhodes

Plate 125: On 9th June 1983, the 08.24 Birmingham to Peterborough service, formed of Etches Park Swindon cross-country set EP528, approaches Ketton. The signal, Ketton box's advance starter, was one of two remaining ex-Midland Railway signals still in use at the time the photograph was taken, (the other being at Leicester). The signal is out of sight of the box and has to be checked regularly to make sure no railway enthusiast has made off with it!

J. Hunns

Plate 126 (Left): Signalling at Manton Junction indicates the importance placed on the main line to Corby when the colour light indicators were installed. Class 25 No. 25289 curves around from the Peterborough direction with the 6M44 Ketton to Castle Bromwich Cement train. Since the revamping of the Birmingham to Norwich service in the mid-1970s, this cross-country route has assumed more importance than the ex-Midland main line through Corby to London.

M. Rhodes

Plate 128 (Right): On 2nd August 1984, a special train of steel coil passes North Kelsey to the south of Barnetby. The coil from Immingham to the Wolverhampton steel terminal is carried on BEV bogie bolster wagons and hauled by Class 31 No. 31163 under the headcode 6Z16.

P. Shannon

Plate 129 (Below Right): In June 1980, the sidings at Mansfield are full of unfitted mineral wagons (MCO and HTO) and BRT grain wagons. Class 56 No. 56008 arrives with the 6G32 empty coal train from High Marnham Power-Station to Mansfield coal concentration depot. A return visit in 1984 found the yard almost empty, with just a couple of merry-go-round trains present; most of the sidings on the left had been removed.

M. Rhodes

Plate 127 (Right): During a downpour at Syston North Junction, near Leicester, Class 37s Nos. 37079 and 37096 pass with a Lackenby to Corby 'Steel-liner'. Twenty loaded BBA bogie bolsters make a total load of 1,500 tons.

M. Rhodes

Plate 130: Back in 1977, many of the Newcastle to Liverpool expresses were hauled by Class 40s. On 8th June 1977, Class 46 No. 46043 was on duty with such a train at Manchester (Victoria).

M. Rhodes

Plate 131: A most unusual view of the Manchester Ship Canal at Latchford to the east of Warrington. A Hertfordshire Railtours' special from London St. Pancras to Amlwch crosses the canal behind Class 45 No. 45111 on the freight-only line which carries merry-go-round trains from Yorkshire to the Fiddlers' Ferry Power-Station.

P. Shannon

Plate 132: At 20.30 on 19th July 1984, the sun is setting at Arnside, as Class 40 No. 40035 trundles over the viaduct with a train of tanks from the Marchon chemical works at Corkickle to Ince and Elton on Merseyside. The Class 40 had spent a couple of days at Workington undergoing minor repairs.

M. Rhodes

Plate 133: A short mixed freight, made up of one STV tube wagon, two 45 ton oil tanks, three CGV grain wagons and a rake of HTV coal hoppers. This Warrington to Healey Mills freight, seen passing Miles Platting behind Class 45 No. 45033, is a potential prototype for the modeller as all the wagons are available either as kits or ready-made items.

M. Rhodes

Plate 134: The ex-Midland railway signal box at Morecambe is unusual in that it is twice the size of the standard Midland railway box. A diesel multiple unit, comprising cars 53610 and 54201, leaves Morecambe with a cross-country service to Leeds on 3rd July 1983.

M. Rhodes

Plate 135: A Carlisle to Barrow passenger train passes through the industrial area to the south of Workington. In a rationalisation plan for the area, the two freight lines on the left are to be removed along with the unusually-named Derwent Haematite Iron Works signal box. Two other signal boxes will also disappear.

M. Rhodes

Plate 136: A light drizzle and morning mist add atmosphere to this picture of the overgrown parcels sidings at Bolton. On 3rd November 1983, Class 40 No. 40096 shunts the 4J17 06.30 Barrow to Red Bank parcels train. In spite of the low light, a 200mm. lens was used at a shutter speed of ¹/₃₀th of a second, the author crouching on the wet rails to hold the camera steady.

M. Rhodes

Plate 137: Another fine study of a Class 40, this time No. 40082, crossing Eskmeals Viaduct on the Cumbrian Coast. The 'Speedlink' service in tow is the 6038 Workington to Dover Town working. Chemicals from Corkickle, and steel rails from Workington, form the load.

P. Shannon

Plate 138: In July 1983, Class 40 No. 40082 passes Workington ironworks with the 8P36 Walton Old Junction to Carlisle freight, which runs via the Cumbrian Coast because of the low maximum speed of unfitted freights (30m.p.h.). Class 08 No. 08078 waits to shunt the train once the Class 40 has parked it in the yard.

M. Rhodes

Plate 139: Leaning on the curve of the West Coast Main Line is Class 40 No. 40150. It is leaving Warrington Arpley Yard with the 6E83 'Speedlink' service to Haverton Hill, on 29th June 1983.

M. Rhodes

Plate 141 (Right): A fine example of a vacuum-braked mixed freight is seen as the 6T34 Ashburys to Hindlow working, passing New Mills South Junction behind Class 40 No. 40184. Shortly after the closure of the Woodhead route, the sidings at Dewsnap were abandoned leaving the tiny yard at Ashburys to cope with all the freight traffic to Greater Manchester.

P. Shannon

Plate 140 (Right): Rounding the sharp corner at Miles Platting comes Class 40 No. 40196 at the head of a variety of wagons from Horwich. The train was running as the 9T54, and on 16th March 1982 it was bound for the now-closed Dewsnap Sidings at Guide Bridge.

M. Rhodes

Plate 142 (Left): Class 25 No. 25106 has to wait for a few moments to enter the Tunstead Sidings, near Buxton, as two Class 37s are approaching from Buxton Shed. The train is the 6H42 08.21 Oakleigh to Tunstead empty stone train, and was photographed at Great Rocks on 7th July 1983.

M. Rhodes

Plate 144 (Right): This scene at Whitehaven Station shows Class 25 No. 25208 drawing 22 loaded HDA hoppers out of the exchange sidings of Haig Colliery. The locomotive will run round the wagons and leave as the 6T36 trip freight bound for Corkickle. Here, two wagon sets will join to form a merry-go-round train to Fiddler's Ferry Power-Station.

M. Rhodes

Plate 145 (Below Right): Class 25s Nos. 25279 and 25323 stand at the head of the 11.45 Widnes to Earles Sidings cement train. At Widnes West Deviation Junction, the main Euston line passes over the freight line from Speke Yard to Warrington.

R. Nelson

Plate 143 (Below): Barrow in Furness once had a thriving network of railway lines around its docks. This has now almost disappeared, the main traffic being coal to the town's coal depots. Hackett coal depot is being shunted by Class 25 No. 25221 on 14th July 1983. Shortly afterwards, it was closed. *P. Shannon*

Plate 146: A crowd of passengers who have just arrived on the train from Wrexham Central watch the arrival of their train to Liverpool at Bidston Dock Station. This example of a 'Merseyside' electric multiple unit has been repainted in the new two-tone livery.

M. Rhodes

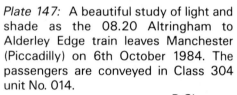

Plate 147: A beautiful study of light and shade as the 08.20 Altringham to Alderley Edge train leaves Manchester (Piccadilly) on 6th October 1984. The passengers are conveyed in Class 304 unit No. 014.

P. Shannon

Plate 148: In the final year of operation of the Class 506 units, cars 59604, 59504 and 59404 pass the crossing keeper's house and the connection to the Dinting Railway Centre, as it approaches Glossop with the 12.13 Hadfield to Manchester train on 16th March 1984.

J. Hunns

Plate 149: Although the East Lancashire line from Preston to Colne is only short, it serves nearly half a million people between these two points. About thirty of the local populace disembark from a diesel multiple unit, comprising cars 51940 and 52057, at Blackburn on 18th July 1981.

M. Rhodes

Plate 152 (Left): A short mixed freight, made up mainly of unfitted MCO mineral wagons, passes west through Guide Bridge Station. The summer sun casts a pattern on the front of Class 25 No. 25249 as it accelerates under the wires on 8th June 1977.

M. Rhodes

Plate 150 (Above Left): The 6P83 Warrington to Blackburn 'Speedlink' freight undertakes a fairly circuitous route between the two yards. Initially it runs to Burscough Bridge, via Wigan, then back to Bolton, where it reverses at Burnden Junction and finally on to Blackburn, via Chorley, and the Faringdon curve. On a wet day in November 1983, Class 47 No. 47106 passes Bolton Station with the 6P83 working.

M. Rhodes

Plate 151 (Below Left): The 6T34 Ashburys to Peak Forest working is pictured arriving at Peak Forest Sidings. The first two wagons, behind Class 37 No. 37201, are classified PAB on the TOPS system, and are bound for Hindlow.

P. Shannon

Plate 153 (Below): One of those lovely 'railway backwater' scenes, captured on 5th July 1983. Class 03 No. 03189 takes an OBA and four SPAs loaded with steel plate to R. Smith's private siding on the Shore Road in Birkenhead. Unfortunately the works was not ready for the load and so it had to return to Cavendish Sidings without delivering the steel.

P. Shannon

Plate 154: Gisburn Tunnel, situated on the Hellifield to Blackburn line, is very rarely photographed. Its impressive portal is used to frame Class 40 No. 40074 on the 5M20 10.14 Perth to Manchester Red Bank vans train. The train was diverted from the West Coast Main Line on 2nd April 1983 because of replacement of a bridge at Tebay.

S. Jolly

Plate 155: The impressive Batty Moss Viaduct at Ribblehead supports the afternoon Carlisle to Leeds 'stopper', hauled by Class 31 No. 31406. Surely British Rail could, with wise investment, make a line of such outstanding beauty a viable commercial proposition.

M. Rhodes

Plate 156: No. 25245 arrives at Chaffers Siding box, Nelson with a single coach officer's special from Manchester on 18th July 1984. The special subsequently returned to Rose Grove before traversing the Copy Pit line to a lunch stop at Hall Royd Junction. Chaffers Siding box marks the start of the single line section from Nelson to the current East Lancs line terminus at Colne.

J. Hunns

Plate 157: On 16th August 1982, a solitary observer watches Class 25 No. 24158 couple up to a train of ballast at Ribblehead. The load is bound for Blackburn.

S. Jolly

Plate 158 (Above Left): On summer Saturdays, a passenger train runs from York to Llandudno. The York portion of the train leaves at 09.00 and is joined on its journey by a portion from Sheffield. Class 25 locomotives Nos. 25153 and 25221 leave the station at Rhyl on their way west on 14th August 1982.

P. Shannon

Plate 159 (Below Left): A train also runs from Llandudno to York on summer Saturdays, leaving the Welsh holiday resort at 09.00 Here, Class 40 No. 40197 heads through Abergele with the train.

P. Shannon

Plate 160 (Above): Class 40 No. 40034 leans on the curve out of Llandudno Junction Station on 29th July 1978. This Manchester (Victoria) to Holyhead working is one of only three trains calling at the station on a very busy Saturday afternoon.

M. Rhodes

Plate 161 (Below): Roadworks are underway for the new North Wales bypass, as Class 47 No. 47104 passes Colwyn Bay Station on 13th August 1982. The train is the 15.45 Manchester (Victoria) to Bangor express.

P. Shannon

Plate 162: Winding their way west past the unusual Chester No. 6 signal box are Class 25s Nos. 25315 and 25286. They are hauling 100 ton oil tanks from Stanlow oil refinery.

K. Fullbrook

Plate 163: Class 47 No. 47340 passes Croess Newydd North Fork Junction with a merry-go-round train from Bersham Colliery, to the south of Wrexham. The train is bound for Fiddler's Ferry Power-Station. Most of the signals on this Great Western bracket are disused and have been since the closure of the GKN steelworks at Brymbo.

M. Rhodes

Plate 164 (Right): The infrequent diesel multiple unit service and the once weekly freight hardly justify the elaborate track layout seen at Whitby on 15th August 1983. A diesel multiple unit, comprising cars 53265 and 54077, form the 15.22 to Darlington, and is seen passing the signal box at Whitby.

P. Shannon

Plate 165 (Above Left): The signal box, crossing gate and home signal all add interest to the picture of the 15.22 Scarborough to Glasgow express. The train passes Strensall at high speed behind Class 37 No. 37013 on 13th July 1984.

M. Rhodes

Plate 166 (Below Left): On Saturday, 24th November 1984, much of the trackwork and signalling at Scarborough was altered. There was only one track in operation which meant that all trains had to reverse out of the station to the carriage sidings before they could run round. Performing just such a manoeuvre is Class 31 No. 31406, which had arrived ten minutes earlier with a train from York.

M. Rhodes

Plate 167 (Above): Old crossing gates and a small country station with an elderly signalman handing over the single line token can still be seen in the 1980s at Bedale, in North Yorkshire. Class 47 No. 47209 passes with the 6P80 Redmire to Redcar stone train on 17th May 1982.

P. Shannon

Plate 168 (Below): The small signal box at Ledston controls the access to Allerton Byewater Colliery, one of the smaller Yorkshire pits producing high-grade coal. Class 47 No. 47089 leaves the pit with the 8K20 freight to Healey Mills Yard.

P. Shannon

Plate 172: A Huddersfield to Sheffield passenger train crosses the impressive viaduct to the north of Penistone Station. A diesel multiple unit comprising cars 51496 and 51431 will travel direct to Sheffield via Nunnery Junction on 29th October 1980. Since the closure of this line the service has run via Barnsley, thus avoiding the need to reverse, and providing a service to the larger population of the Barnsley area.

M. Rhodes

Plate 173: A diesel multiple unit, formed of cars 50257 and 56090, departs from Ilkley with the 17.05 service to Leeds, on 21st July 1982.

P. Shannon

Plate 174: The sidings at York North Yard are used to stage trainloads of coal from the Durham Coalfield to the Aire Valley Power-Stations. Here, on 30th August 1985, Class 56 No. 56114 eases south with a train for Drax Power-Station, as Class 37s Nos. 37100 and 37009 arrive with the 7L70 13.37 Easington to York merry-go-round service.
M. Rhodes

Plate 175: Class 56 No. 56034 passes Burton Salmon Junction with a southbound merry-go-round train on 11th August 1981. In the background the 6E40 10.18 Rylstone to Hull stone train disappears behind Class 31s Nos. 31188 and 31409.
P. Shannon

Plate 176: An unfitted freight from Tinsley to Dewsnap winds its way along the Woodhead route at Dunford Bridge. On 18th June 1981, this working was hauled by Class 76 No. 76035.

P. Shannon

Plate 177: The 1 in 40 gradient of the Worsborough Incline is clearly seen in this picture. Two Class 76s, Nos. 76007 and 76026, head the 6M55 Wath Yard to Fiddler's Ferry Power-Station merry-go-round working, whilst Nos. 76006 and 76024 bring up the rear. The banking engines were attached at Wombwell Junction and will help the train all the way to Barnsley Junction at Penistone. The train was travelling at about 15m.p.h. as it passed Kendall Green Crossing on 4th March 1981.

M. Rhodes

Plate 178 (Left): On the first day of regular locomotive haulage between Sheffield and Hull (13th May 1984), Class 31 No. 31406 joins the main Leeds to Hull line at Gilberdyke Junction. The line to the left from Goole is threatened with closure because of expensive repairs which are needed near the swing bridge at Goole.
M. Rhodes

Plate 180 (Right): In July 1983, Class 47 No. 47001 is caught in the beautiful surroundings of Kirkham Abbey. The train is the 11.23 (Saturdays only) Bangor to Scarborough holiday service.
S. Jolly

Plate 179 (Below Left): An unusual sight at Treeton Junction on 23rd September 1980 was Class 25 No. 25097 speeding past with empty coaching stock bound for York.
M. Rhodes

Plate 181 (Below): The 07.05 Plymouth to Leeds express passes Goose Hill Junction to the south of Normanton. An HST, with power cars 43188 and 43187, has travelled north on the old Midland main line via Cudworth. Inter-City services on the NE/SW corridor have subsequently been diverted via Moorethorpe, and in May 1984, several were routed via Doncaster, even further east.
P. Shannon

Plate 182: A reminder of how rapidly our rail network is changing. In October 1980, only four years ago, Class 76s Nos. 76021 and 76008 pass Penistone at the head of the 8M17 Wath to Ashburys freight. Since this picture was taken, revenue-earning freights have become entirely air-braked, all the Class 76s have been withdrawn, and the Woodhead route has been closed, the section of line from Wath to Penistone having been lifted by the beginning of 1984.

M. Rhodes

Plate 183: A trio of freights are seen parked at Healey Mills. From left to right are Class 47 No. 47252 with the 6Z12 ICI Burn Naze to Haverton Hill working, Class 56 No. 56093 at the end of its journey on the 6E33 Fiddler's Ferry to Healey Mills freight and Class 37s Nos. 37202 and 37160 with the 6E60 Preston to Lindsey empty oil train.

M. Rhodes

Plate 184: Class 37 No. 37119 prepares to leave Knottingley with a rake of PAA hoppers bound initially for Doncaster Decoy Yard. From here they will return to Middleton Towers near King's Lynn to pick up more sand for Pilkington's glassworks in Knottingley.

M. Rhodes

Plate 185: A varied load of ferry wagons and steel wagons leaves Tinsley Yard behind two Class 20s, Nos. 20003 and 20066, on 23rd September 1980. The train is the 9T34 trip to the Sheffield freight terminal. Since this picture was taken the terminal in Sheffield has been rationalised to handle only steel, rather than general merchandise.

M. Rhodes

Plate 186 (Left): The large station at Bradford (Forster Square), which used to host expresses to Scotland and the north country, can now only manage stored Eastern Region 'Ilford' electric multiple units. These are disturbed only by the hourly local service to either Keighley or Ilkley. Here, a diesel multiple unit, formed of cars 78959 and 78709, departs for Keighley on 13th May 1984.

M. Rhodes

Plate 188 (Right): On 10th October 1983, the sun reflects off the wet tracks in Blyth West Yard. Class 08 No. 08255 waits for the afternoon shift to arrive before it pushes another load of coal up to the staithes and into a waiting ship.

M. Rhodes

Plate 187: A panorama of the western approaches to Leeds Station photographed from the Dragonara Hotel in June 1977. Class 45 No. 45127 winds its way into the station as No. 45118 leaves. Class 46 No. 46055 and Class 47 No. 47525 can be seen at the stabling point on the left.

M. Rhodes

Plate 191 (Right): This view of Darlington Depot was photographed from the station using a 500mm. telephoto lens. Darlington depot maintains all the diesel multiple units used on the many north-eastern secondary services. On 11th February 1984, two units pause between duties.

M. Rhodes

Plate 192 (Below Right): The name of Norton East signal box is partially obscured by the shutters which are only removed when the box is open during the morning shift. A Middlesborough to Newcastle train passes in the hands of a diesel multiple unit, comprising cars 53171 and 53248, on 13th October 1983.

M. Rhodes

Plate 189 (Above): A Class 101 diesel multiple unit, made up of cars 53193, 59085 and 53162, passes the remains of the former Hartlepool Steelworks with the 12.56 Middlesbrough to Newcastle service on 16th March 1985.

J. Hunns

Plate 190 (Below): Horden Colliery provides a panoramic backdrop for a Darlington to Newcastle train formed of a 2-car diesel multiple unit.

M. Rhodes

Plate 193 (Above): Photographed back in June 1980, when Consett Steelworks was still in full production, Class 37s Nos. 37007 and 37001 pass Consett High Yard with a train of iron ore from Redcar.

M. Rhodes

Plate 194 (Below): This photograph, taken on 10th May 1982, provides quite a contrast to the picture above. Class 37 No. 37094 passes Carr House, near Consett High Yard with MCVs loaded with scrap and bound for Tyne Yard. The derelict steelworks can be seen in the background.

P. Shannon

Plate 195: The daily load of scrap from Millfield scrap works, at Stockton, shunts in the overgrown sidings adjacent to the station on 13th October 1983. Class 37 No. 37098 will take the train to Tees Yard.

M. Rhodes

Plate 196: On 5th November 1981, a derailment on the East Coast Main Line caused the diversion of several services including the 4E36 Workington to Lackenby steel train, seen passing Penshaw. Class 31s Nos. 31301 and 31186 bring back the empty wagons which have taken steel billets to the Workington plant where they are fashioned into steel rails.

P. Shannon

Plate 197: Passing the half-empty gantries at North Shore is Class 47 No. 47302. The train is the 7N40 Leeds ORT to Port Clarence empty oil tanks and was photographed on 13th October 1983.

M. Rhodes

Plate 199: An HST, with power cars 43093 and 43121, accelerates past Ouston Junction with a King's Cross to Edinburgh service. Meanwhile, Class 47 No. 47129 waits for a path on to the main line with its freight, the 4M77 Bathgate to Washwood Heath working. This service returns empty carriages to the BL plant at Longbridge.

M. Rhodes

Plate 198 (Left): Belasis Lane is the junction between the freight line to the Port Clarence oil refineries and the sidings in ICI's Haverton Hill complex. Passing the box, on 14th October 1983, is Class 47 No. 47301 at the head of the 6049 Haverton Hill to Eastleigh 'Speedlink' service.

M. Rhodes

Plate 200 (Right). Another view at Ouston Junction, on the evening of 19th August 1985, shows Class 47 No. 47224 arriving at Tyne Yard with the 6S46 Healey Mills to Mossend 'Speedlink' service. The coal in containers is bound for G.J. Russell & Co. who distribute the loads from their depot at Gaitcosh, near Glasgow.

M. Rhodes

Plate 201: This 1978 view at Newcastle shows Class 55 'Deltic' No. 55015 *Tulyar* arriving from the north with an Edinburgh to King's Cross express.

M. Rhodes

Plate 202: On Sundays, the 16.37 King's Cross to Newcastle express travels north to Tyne and Wear via the 'capital' of Teeside, Middlesborough. Seen here on 14th August 1983 crossing Yarm Viaduct are HST power cars Nos. 43112 and 43122.

J. Hunns

Plate 203 (Above): A train loaded with coal, bound for the staithes at Jarrow, winds its way out of Derwenthaugh Exchange Sidings behind Class 37 No. 37003 on 11th October 1983. Because of motive power problems that morning, the train was only travelling as far as Tyne Yard from where it would be 'tripped' to Wardley Exchange Sidings later in the day.

M. Rhodes

Plate 204 (Below): In October 1983, friends in the north-east had suggested that the line from Butterwell directly to Ashington was disused. The author's suspicion was aroused by finding the rails in a relatively shiny state. Several hours later Class 37 No. 37153 was photographed passing Ashington Colliery with a train of coal from Butterwell loading point to Blyth West Yard.

M. Rhodes

Plate 205: After the line from Blyth had been closed for several hours because of engineering work, on 4th September 1985, Class 37 No. 37062 arrives at Ashington with a lengthy load of empty coal hoppers.

M. Rhodes

Plate 206: Dawdon Colliery is situated eight miles south of Sunderland, perched on the cliffs overlooking the North Sea. Class 37 No. 37033 passes the appropriately-named Seabanks signal box whilst shunting in the colliery on 14th October 1983.

M. Rhodes

Plate 207: The 13.08 (Sundays only) Heaton to Red Bank empty parcels train is routed over the Leamside line. On 18th October 1981, the train is seen passing Fence Houses signal box behind Class 40 No. 40141.

P. Shannon

Plate 208: Sadly, the delightful little signal box at Wolsingham no longer exists. The driver of Class 37 No. 37172 has just collected the single line token from the signalman as it winds its way towards the main line with the 6K70 Eastgate to Heaton cement train.

P. Shannon

Plate 211 (Right): New-liveried Class 20 No. 20227 shunts at Cameron Bridge on 2nd May 1986. Its load of two CO_2 tanks have come from Thornton Yard as the 6G04 freight, and will be discharged into the large cylinder in the background.

M. Rhodes

Plate 209: Super power for the Workington to Lackenby empty steel train on 23rd November 1984. Class 56s Nos. 56124 and 56134 accelerate south past Lamesley after a two hour wait in Tyne Yard for a driver. The crew of the north-bound Haverton Hill to Leith anhydrous ammonia train take the 'Steel-liner' on the last leg of its journey to Teesside.

M. Rhodes

Plate 210 (Below): One of the few remaining regular trip workings for a Class 03 shunter in 1983 was the trip from Tyne Yard to Low Fell, Dunston and Blaydon coal depot. At the western extremity of its trip is Class 03 No. 03094, shunting in Blaydon coal depot.

M. Rhodes

Scotland

Plate 212: Class 26 No. 26024 enters Dingwall on a beautiful summer morning in 1981. The train is the 07.00 Kyle of Lochalsh to Inverness working.

M. Rhodes

Plate 213: An Edinburgh to Aberdeen express descends from the Tay Bridge at the Dundee end. Class 47 No. 47268 coasts past the signal box west of Dundee on 24th March 1981.

M. Rhodes

Plate 214: Deep in the hollow hewn out to build Glasgow (Queen Street) Station is Class 27 No. 27101. It awaits departure with the 12.30 Glasgow to Edinburgh 'push-pull' express on 8th July 1978.

M. Rhodes

Plate 215: The 10.30 'Clansman' Inverness to London (Euston) express accelerates out of Inverness past the impressive signal gantries controlled by Welsh's Bridge signal box. Class 47 No. 47467 has a hard climb ahead to haul its twelve coaches up to Culloden Moor.

M. Rhodes

Plate 216: A train of empty mineral wagons (MCV) joins the main line to Ayr at Barassie. The train has come from the Kilmarnock direction and is bound for the yard at Newton on Ayr. The panel signal box on the right of the locomotive must signify the imminent demise of the fine semaphore signals at Barassie.

K. Fullbrook

Plate 217: Class 27 No. 27014 passes the goods yard at Dumfries with a 'down' parcels train. It is, in fact, the IS40 05.13 London (Euston) to Stranraer Harbour mail train, and was photographed on 26th July 1985.

P. Shannon

Plate 218: On 22nd June 1982, crossing locomotives are captured on film at Grangemouth. Class 20 No. 20089 hauls a southbound mixed freight whilst Class 37 No. 37007 returns light engine to Grangemouth Shed.

P. Shannon

Plate 219: The old station signs at Newton on Ayr add interest to this view of Class 27 No. 27212 hauling a rake of HBAs from Ayr Harbour to the Ayrshire Coalfield. This locomotive was used on the Edinburgh to Glasgow 'push-pull' services five years ago.

P. Shannon

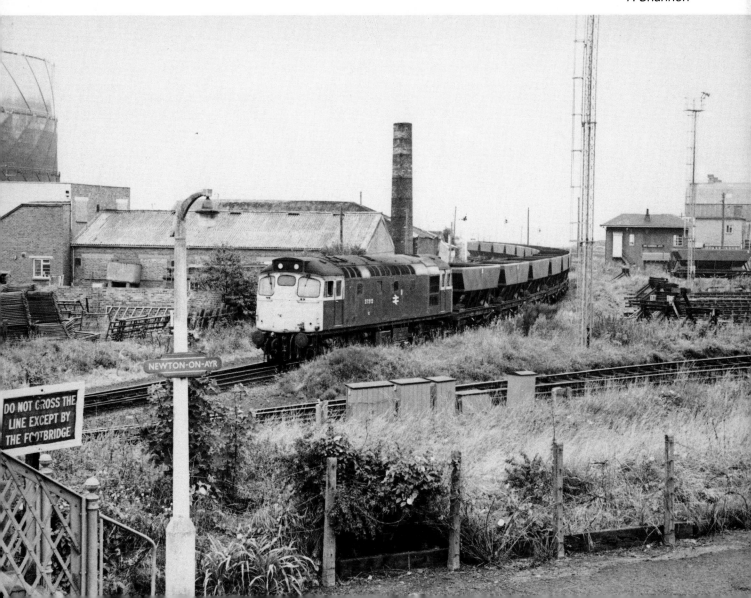

Plate 220: On 27th August 1981, the afternoon train from Mallaig arrives at Fort William with an observation car first in the formation, behind Class 37 No. 37081.

P. Shannon

Plate 221: This intriguing and highly original view shows the morning Fort William to Glasgow train approaching Corrour. Class 37 No. 37112 appears to be hauling its train straight out of the ground on this sunny morning in August 1981.

P. Shannon

Plate 222: Inverness Station is the setting for this view of Class 40 No. 40167 at the head of a summer extra from Inverness to Edinburgh. The summer of 1979 was really the last summer when the Class 40s hauled the majority of the expresses over the Highland main line. By 1980, Class 47s had taken over most of the trains.
M. Rhodes

Plate 223: Class 27s Nos. 27208 and 27108 leave Edinburgh (Waverley) with a mid-morning 'push-pull' express to Glasgow. Since this picture was taken on 10th July 1978, the service has been handed over to the Class 47/7 locomotives. Many of the Class 27s which used to haul these hourly expresses are now confined to more mundane duties on local freights in Scotland.
M. Rhodes

Plate 224: The clouds roll over the hills to the south of Invergordon as two Class 26s arrive with the 11.10 Inverness to Wick train. The postman waits with his barrow and parcels for Class 26s Nos. 26027 and 26039 to come to a halt. The second Class 26 was needed further north at Georgemas Junction to replace a failed Class 26 on the Thurso branch.

M. Rhodes

Plate 225: A general view of Thurso Station and goods yard includes Class 26 No. 26042 at the head of the Thurso portion of the tea time departure for Inverness. Various passengers can be seen on the platform boarding what is the last departure of the day.

M. Rhodes

Plate 226: The morning sun breaks through the clouds at Inverness to highlight the magnificent ex-Highland Railway signal bracket which controls the northern approaches to the station. Class 37 No. 37183 arrives with the early morning train from Wick, on 14th August 1982.
M. Rhodes

Plate 227: The 'new order' on the far north line, with Class 37 No. 37035 at the head of the 11.10 Wick to Inverness passenger train. The train was photographed on 5th August 1982 at Conon Bridge.
S. Jolly

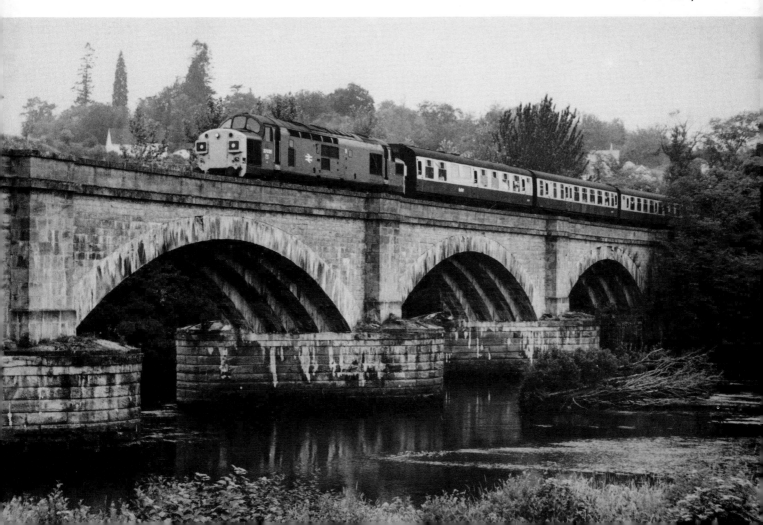

Plate 228 (Left): Class 20 No. 20119 heads a train of empty bitumen tanks down the harbour branch at Ardrossan. The ruins of Ardrossan Castle stand high above the branch line. After loading, the tanks will form an evening departure to Culloden Moor, near Inverness. *P. Shannon*

Plate 230 (Right): Having rejoined the Inverness to Aberdeen main line at Alves, Class 40 No. 40006 passes the closed station at Alves. The empty BRT grain hoppers are on their way from Burghead to Doncaster. *S. Jolly*

Plate 231 (Below Right): A single Class 20 locomotive, No. 20156, curves south from Stirling with an unidentified train of chemical tanks on 19th March 1984. *J. Hunns*

Plate 229 (Below): A local trip freight from Stirling to Grangemouth Yard accelerates south under a fine array of signals at Stirling on 19th July 1984. Class 20s Nos. 20011 and 20097 have four fuel oil tanks and a four engineer's wagons in tow.

P. Shannon

Plate 232: Class 27 No. 27059 collects the single line token for the Menstrie branch at Cambus Junction, Alloa. On 12th May 1986, the 6NO6 trip from Grangemouth has three 'polybulks' carrying grain from Royston to Cambus, and eight TTA tanks with molasses from York to Menstrie.

M. Rhodes

Plate 233: A busy scene at Falkland Junction, Newton on Ayr. Class 27 No. 27210 arrives with a train of empty mineral wagons whilst Class 20 No. 20118 shunts what will be a north-bound fitted freight.

J. Hunns